Lectio Divina
And the
Practice of Teresian Prayer

Sam Anthony Morello, OCD

About the Author

Sam Anthony Morello, OCD, is a priest of the Southwestern (St. Thérèse) Province of Discalced Carmelites, where he has served as novice master, student master, provincial councilor, provincial delegate to the Secular Carmelites, and Director of the Mt. Carmel Center in Dallas, Texas. In 1991 he completed a term as Definitor (Councilor) at the Discalced Carmelite Generalate in Rome, Italy.

Lectio Divina
And the
Practice of Teresian Prayer

Sam Anthony Morello, OCD

An ICS Pamphlet

ICS Publications
Institute of Carmelite Studies
Washington, D.C.
1995

(This article originally appeared in the Summer 1991 issue of *Spiritual Life*.)

ICS Publications
2131 Lincoln Road NE
Washington, DC 20002–1199

Typeset and produced in the U.S.A.

Cover Woodcut by Robert F. McGovern

Library of Congress Cataloging-in-Publication Data

Morello, Sam Anthony, 1934–.
    Lectio divina and the practice of Teresian prayer /
Sam Anthony Morello
        p. cm. — (An ICS pamphlet)
        Includes bibliographical references.
        ISBN: 0–935216–24–3
        1. Prayer—Catholic Church. 2. Teresa of Avila, Saint, 1515–1582.
3. Carmelites—Spiritual life. 4. Bible—Devotional Use.
I. Title. II. Title: Lectio divina. III. Series.
BV215.M7   1994
242'.802—dc20   94–28368
                                                CIP

Contents

Abbreviations

All quotations from St. Teresa of Jesus are taken from *The Collected Works of St. Teresa of Avila*, trans. Kieran Kavanaugh and Otilio Rodriguez, 3 vols. (Washington, DC: ICS Publications, 1976–1985). For her major works, the following abbreviations are used:

> *Castle* = Interior Castle
> *Foundations* = Book of Foundations
> *Life* = Book of Her Life
> *Way* = Way of Perfection

The two numbers ordinarily following references to the *Foundations, Life,* and *Way* refer to the chapter and section in the ICS editions. Since the *Interior Castle* is divided into seven "dwelling places," references to the *Castle* include an additional first number, identifying the "dwelling places" in which a chapter and section may be found. Thus "*Life,* 8, 5" refers to the fifth section of the eighth chapter of the *Book of Her Life,* while "*Castle,* 6, 7, 10" refers to the sixth "dwelling places," chapter 7, section 10.

Lectio Divina
and the
Practice of Teresian Prayer

By Sam Anthony Morello, OCD

Introduction

To approach the subject of Teresian prayer (that is, prayer
after the pattern of St. Teresa of Avila) we need a broad perspective. This is necessary, although perhaps surprising, because there
is no distinctively Teresian way to pray. There is not even a uniquely
Carmelite way to pray. Carmel's spirituality is rooted in the greater
tradition of *lectio divina* (literally, "divine reading"), a particular way
of reading and praying over the Scriptures. This is why we read at
the very heart of the Carmelite *Rule* of St. Albert: "Each one of you
is to stay in his own cell or nearby, *pondering the Law of the Lord* [i.e.,
sacred Scripture] *day and night and keeping watch at his prayers* unless
attending to some other duty" (*Rule*, no. 8).

Pondering sacred Scripture was the way the early monks, the
desert fathers and mothers, and in fact the people of the bible,
prayed. And the monks developed a traditional method for doing
that, the ingredients of which we find rehearsed in John of the Cross

when he writes: "Seek in *reading* and you will find in *meditation;* knock in *prayer* and it will be opened to you in *contemplation*" *(Sayings,* #158).[1]

We will see how those four elements of *lectio* perfectly serve Teresian prayer, or better said, how the Teresian approach to prayer serves *lectio.* But let us first examine some underlying Teresian notions and principles, looking at Teresa's methods and her preferred prayer orientation, as well as her understanding of the goals of prayer. All of these might be called Teresian "attitudes," wonderfully helpful attitudes that enrich the monastic tradition of prayer and can broaden contemporary approaches to prayer.

Teresian Notions

Mental Prayer. Teresa's understanding of prayer is a good place to begin. We may simply recall what she says about prayer in chapter eight of her autobiography: "Mental prayer in my opinion is nothing else than an intimate sharing between friends; it means taking time frequently to be alone with him who we know loves us" (*Life*, 8, 5).[2] This puts prayer in the category of friendship. Clearly, it is God who has initiated the friendship; thus personal prayer is a response to a love already shown us by the God of revelation. One goes to prayer as to someone whose love for us is assured; the one praying answers the voice of benevolence and love in return. This implies that prayer is an art to be cultivated, for it requires often setting time aside to attend to the friend. As we shall see, the friend is Jesus Christ, the center of the entire Teresian system.

The notion of prayer as a response to friendship gratuitously offered us by God through Christ is rooted in St. John's Gospel. It is important, as John teaches, that we not pray to *win* God's favor and love; God has *already* loved us most personally in Christ. What we need to do is answer that love. Thus prayer is an aspect of the life of grace. Graced prayer receives the love of God for the self and returns it in two ways: by loving God directly and by loving our brothers and sisters in God and for God. Prayer is "agape" received for personal transformation and then channeled back to God and out to neighbor. The very nature of evangelical and Teresian prayer spells out its goals. In sum, prayer is a loving exchange with Christ.

Vocal Prayer. Now let us see what Teresa means when she speaks of "vocal prayer." In a word, vocal prayer is nothing but formulary prayer, praying a pre-fabricated set of words and sentiments, like the "Our Father" or a psalm. The saint wants us to say our prayers well! She asks that we repeat the words "with understanding." She wants us to say our prayers "attentively." Reciting our vocal prayers well is already "mental prayer"; there is no distinction between mental and vocal prayer when vocal prayer is truly made one's own (see *Way*, 24). For Teresa the first lesson in learning to meditate is to say one's vocal prayers with attention and affection.

Meditation. It is helpful here to take a look at the term "meditation" in the Teresian writings. Teresa uses the word in reference to several prayerful activities that all qualify as ascetical prayer or "meditation." This is the first thing to note, that "meditation" for Teresa is a *category* of prayer. It is the prayer of effort, effort to think about and love the Lord. Meditation is all prayer this side of contemplation; it is the prayer of the first three dwelling-places of the *Interior Castle* and of the first waters of the *Life.*

With that understood, let us look at some specific applications of the term "meditation" in the saint's writings. At the outset of the *Interior Castle* we read that "the door to the castle is prayer and reflection" (*Castle*, 1, 1, 7). *Reflection* is the first meaning of meditation for St. Teresa, and she gives many examples of "much discursive reflection with the intellect" (see *Castle*, 6, 7, 10). The use of the imagination, reasoning, and will at prayer are all discursive meditative activities.

It is also "meditation" to devoutly follow the prayer outline of a meditation book. "There are books in which the mysteries of the Lord's life and passion are divided according to the days of the week, and there are meditations on judgment, hell, our nothingness, and the many things we owe God together with excellent doctrine and method concerning the beginning and the end of prayer" (*Way*, 19, 1). Teresa is open to this reflective use of a planned meditation book for those who find it helpful.

Teresa calls the active *prayer of recollection* "an excellent kind of meditation" (*Castle*, 4, 3, 3). It is a style of meditation that locates the presence of God within the self and centers all reflection and affection on God there. This was a favorite prayer "method" for Teresa (see, for example, *Way*, 29, 7), as we will indicate in more detail below.

A surprising reference to meditation is found in Teresa's treatment of a passive form of the *prayer of recollection*. She tells us that when we begin to experience the first degree of infused contemplation (i.e., the passive prayer of recollection), "meditation, or the work of the intellect must not be put aside" (*Castle*, 4, 3, 8). Here we are dealing with a "mixed prayer" in the Teresian system, a borderline state midway between meditation and the first really strong contemplative experience (the prayer of quiet). When one is given a less powerful form of contemplation in the "passive prayer of recollection," he or she may gently continue to recite vocal prayers, repeat a biblical word, or quietly reflect, as a method of maintaining receptivity and responsiveness to the infusion. Such personal activity for Teresa is meditative, and could be applied to any form of contemplative prayer experience that leaves the faculties free.

To sum up, meditation is basically a category of non-contemplative prayer, the stage of prayer that presumes the ordinary use of our mental powers in searching for God, though always under the guidance of divine grace.[3]

Teresian Characteristics and Attitudes

Attention. Next we look at some characteristics of Teresian prayer. The first thing to note is that for Teresa prayer must be "mental" to be prayer at all. She means that our exercise of prayer needs to be *attentive.* She is realistic enough to give plenty of space to the subject of natural distractions, but on the level of conviction and effort she wants us to pray carefully and attentively. Often she uses the term "mental prayer," so common in her day, to designate "private" or personal prayer. She explains that mental prayer is a matter of "being aware and knowing that we are speaking, with whom we are speaking, and who we ourselves are who dare to speak so much with so great a Lord." Without such awareness and attention to what we say, our prayer is mere "gibberish" (*Way*, 25, 3). So prayer demands presence to ourselves, to what we think and say, and to Christ to whom we speak in response. Teresian prayer is "mental," presence to presence, and the essence of this presence is the memory of Christ.

Affection. Teresian prayer is characteristically *affective.* Everybody knows Teresa's insistence that the "important thing" in prayer "is not to think much but to love much" (*Castle,* 4, 1, 7; cf. *Foundations,* 5, 2). In the same place St. Teresa gives us her primary principle: "Do what best stirs you to love." The primary reason for praying is affective communion with God. Everything moves in Teresian prayer toward affective rapport with Christ and his Father in the Spirit. The strong affective orientation she gives to prayer has contemplation in mind; through affective simplicity one best disposes oneself for the gift of contemplation.

Affective prayer is communion with God, a communion leading to union. Union with God is the goal of prayer for Teresa. Affectivity opens the way to communion and union. Teresian prayer is essentially affective, and the essence of affectivity is desire, the desire for God. Whether or not it is felt on an emotional level, true affectivity lies in the desire for personal union with the beloved.

Christ and the Virtues. Teresian prayer is characteristically Christ-centered. Christ is the direct object of both the mental and the affective dynamics of Teresian prayer. Teresa prays with, to, and through Jesus Christ. Her Christ is the Christ of the Gospels; Christ as the "Way, the Truth, and the Life" is her constant focus. That focus must be learned by the beginner, retained by those advanced in prayer, and refined into a "loving gaze" by the contemplative (see *Life,* 12 and 22, and *Castle,* 6, 7 for Teresa's classic treatment of the essential role of Christ in every stage of the ascent of prayer). Some of her principles in this area are that: 1) meditation's best subject and object is the biblical Christ in his life, death, and resurrection; 2) one's prayer is best habitually (though not exclusively) centered on Christ; 3) the sacred humanity of Christ is the most adequate mediation for initial growth in prayer and the best assurance of and preparation for the gift of contemplation; and 4) any other opinion is gravely suspect and harmful.

Teresa, our teacher, knows how important the figure of Christ is to the one who prays. Christ is a friend and companion at prayer (see *Way*, 26, 1). Christ addresses the loneliness of the meditator. He fills the void, thus turning loneliness into solitude and access to God. Furthermore, the Christ of Scripture is the model of all the virtues that we desire to learn. After all, Christian perfection lies in the virtues. We pray to be transformed; transformation is brought about in the first instance by the acquisition of the virtues, which then open us up to the further deification of contemplation and the states of union. We need Christ to train us in the theological and cardinal virtues. Unless we strive after the virtues we "will always be dwarfs" (*Castle*, 7, 4, 9). And since charity and humility give birth to all the other virtues, we desperately need the living model of Jesus Christ, the humble one, to show us the way. "This whole building ...has humility as its foundation," and to build Christian humility we must "fix our eyes on the Crucified" (*Castle*, 7, 4, 8). With Christ as our friend and teacher we will be drawn all the way into the bosom of the Blessed Trinity (see *Castle*, 6, 7, 7).[4]

The Contemplative Dimension. Teresian prayer is oriented toward contemplation. This is another essential quality to appreciate. For St. Teresa, meditation is ascetical prayer; that is, it depends on our efforts as we exercise our faculties with the help of ordinary grace. Contemplation cannot be produced by our efforts; it is completely gratuitous. We can dispose ourselves for it by the virtues and by praying in a very simplified affective way. But contemplation is an infused experience of the presence of God that gives light to the soul and warmth to the heart. As a habit it begins in the fourth dwelling-places with the experience of passive recollection; it then flowers into the prayer of quiet.

Nonetheless we can say in a certain sense that all Teresian prayer is contemplative. What we mean is that Teresa always has her mind's eye on contemplation even if she is giving the very first lessons in the attentive recitation of vocal prayer. Teresa teaches us to desire contemplation explicitly; we learn even to ask for it while surrendering the outcome to God. But when we pray in the Teresian spirit, we pray *open* to contemplation. We learn to listen to the

Word of God, receptive to God's action of love and light, gently dwelling on the presence of Christ found in Scripture. We do not work hard at it; we leave much room for God to work. We learn to be still in the presence, to return to our source in Christ, as we "chew" the Word of God. That leisurely attitude, when coupled with sincerity, opens our depths to the mystical action of God. At times a person experiences the very meaning of the words he or she is saying. At times one is flooded with understanding, with new energy or resolve, with a fanned flame of love for God and neighbor. That type of prayer is clearly *received*, so effortless and elevating that it qualifies as contemplation. Contemplation is *given* prayer, the Spirit praying in us. Contemplation is "seeing beyond believing," as Augustine once put it. Contemplation is being pulled into the mind and heart of Christ who knows the Father in the clarity of the Spirit and surrenders all to him. Contemplation is "supernatural" prayer, according to Teresa, for it "cannot be acquired by effort or diligence, however much one tries, although one can dispose oneself for it which would help a great deal" (*Spiritual Testimonies*, 58, 3). Why desire it and why pray in such a way as to be sensitive to its calling? Because contemplation is a "short cut" to the perfection of the virtues and to union with God (See *Castle*, 5, 3, 4). In summary, *Teresian prayer is contemplative* in that it desires contemplation, aims at contemplation, is open to contemplation. In this sense even Teresian meditation is contemplative.

Teresian Methods

Vocal Prayer. Let us attempt at this point to name the major methods and activities of meditative prayer that St. Teresa discusses for our instruction. First on our list is *vocal prayer*. This is an important subject. Teresa clearly sees that vocal prayer can sustain any kind of meditative effort. And in this she joins company with the monastic centuries that based prayer on biblical texts, as Teresa does on the Lord's Prayer in the *Way of Perfection*. The first lesson in prayer for Teresa is learning to say vocal prayers well with attention, and identifying with their sentiments. We shall see that the rediscovery of monastic "lectio" would reinstate the biblical word as the basis of Christian meditation. Somehow Teresa remains in touch with that basic methodology. She is clear that vocal prayer serves not only meditation but contemplation as well: "I know that there are many persons who while praying vocally...are raised by God to sublime contemplation.... It's because of this that I insist so much, daughters, upon your reciting vocal prayer well" (*Way*, 30, 7; cf. *Way*, 24, passim).

Reading. Second, we list *reading*. Apart from the practice of following a book with meditation outlines, Teresa also treats of praying with a book for the whole time of prayer. She asserts that it is "a great help to take a good book written in the vernacular in order to recollect one's thoughts and pray well vocally..." (*Way*, 26, 10). But she goes even further, reaffirming again the whole monastic tradition of prayer: "I have always been fond of the words of the Gospels...and found more recollection in them than in very cleverly written books" (*Way*, 21, 3).[5] It is the Bible that provides the best book for private prayer. The best way to feed prayer is to ponder the words of Scripture. Carmelites (in fact, all Christians) make a great mistake in trying to practice "the presence of God" without sustaining it by the word of God. We need to learn to pray over God's word. Let's not miss the relation between Teresa's teaching on vocal prayer and her thoughts on praying over a book. St. Teresa uses the words of Scripture for vocal prayer. The "Our Father" is given as one example, not to limit the use of other passages. *Any* sentence or phrase or word of scripture, repeated over and over or recited very carefully, is vocal prayer; and that word or vocal prayer is drawn from her favorite book, the Gospels. In short, Teresa's teachings on vocal prayer and on the use of the Gospels come together in the practice of "praying over the Scriptures." This makes for a most substantial prayer life.

Images. The recollected use of *sacred images* comes next on our list of prayer methods. Teresa encourages us to look at "an image or painting of this Lord" that is to our "liking" so as "to speak often to Him" (*Way*, 26, 9). Here we have a helpful method for practicing the presence of God. The use of good images and icons (which the Orthodox venerate so devoutly) is an excellent practice. Fortified by the word of Scripture and the image of Christ we are ready to pray. Our senses must learn to serve our prayer rather than distract from it. In her *Life* (ch. 9) we see how images were especially helpful to Teresa because of her difficulty in picturing what she had never seen. The principle, however, is very broad. Sacred images are good for people with poor imaginations or good imaginations. But images must have an appeal to the person before they can be of inspirational value; some people do not profit from images, or do not need them. Sacred images can most certainly serve individual prayer, just as they serve liturgical prayer in our churches.

Imaginative representations must be named on our list. "I strove to picture Christ within me, and it did me greater good—in my opinion—to picture Him in those scenes where I saw Him more alone" (*Life*, 9, 4). A holy imagination enables us to really identify with scriptural scenes, as Teresa did. A playful but disciplined imagination is essential to the classical prayer tradition. Interior images can serve prayer as effectively as exterior ones. But images, like discursive reflections, must nourish affection. Images are means, and good ones when they feed the heart and the will. We would do well to allow images and feelings mature expression within us as we encounter them in the Scriptures and in other books and pious exercises that serve our prayer. Images can put us in touch with ourselves as few other things can. Biblical images have special power for this, and we need to trust our own spontaneous images triggered by the biblical images. Images help us to get in touch with feelings; our feelings need to be redeemed, purified, and elevated by the word of God. The prudent and inspired use of our faculties is enhanced and facilitated immensely when we are in touch with our images, memories, and feelings. We certainly have the impression that St. Teresa was in touch with hers. Mature images of nature and grace easily mediate the presence of God.

Reflection, Intuition, and Self-Knowledge. Reflection has already been named as an element of Teresian meditation. We briefly include it here, and associate thinking, understanding, and evaluating with it.

There is a more "right-brain" kind of knowing called *intuition* that we must also mention; briefly, it involves dwelling on a biblical text or image with a loving gaze, gently looking at God, rather than studying or working with the analytical mind. The ability to dwell rather than dig is the heart of affective prayer, so characteristically Teresian. Simple intuition breeds the simplicity of love. Teresa explains herself very clearly here; she advises us to stop working so hard, to take a "Sabbath," some time off. She tells us not to tire the intellect, but just to "speak with and delight in Him and not wear ourselves out in composing syllogisms." Such acts, she assures us, "contain a great amount of sustenance" (*Life*, 13, 11). In this sense she leads us to simply *look* at him who looks at us: "I'm not asking...that you draw out a lot of concepts or make long and subtle reflections with your intellect. I'm not asking you to do anything more than look at Him" (*Way*, 26, 3). This "looking" is intuitive.

While speaking of thinking and intuiting, we ought to include reference to the meditative asceticism of *self-knowledge*, to which Teresa devotes so many pages. She clearly perceives the importance of walking in self-knowledge all the days of our life (see *Castle*, 1, 2, 8). Teresa does not advocate self-consciousness, but she most assuredly wants self-awareness; not self-centeredness, but transcendent self-presence (to steal a notion from Father Adrian van Kaam). This is but a matter of humility for Teresa; otherwise we cannot "walk in the truth" (*Castle*, 6, 10). We need to understand our own inner powers (see her interest in the natural workings of the imagination in *Castle*, 4, 1), as well as our own temperament (see what she says about the melancholy person in *Foundations*, 7). We need to compare the inner darkness (the demonic or shadow self) with the light and brightness of our Lord (see *Castle*, 1, 2). Humility and self-knowledge are one and the same for Teresa (see *Castle*, 1, 2). Unless we walk in the radical truth about ourselves we will not know the truth about God either. And unless we walk in truth we are not pleasing to God. With a precision like that of Thomas Aquinas, Teresa perceives that unless we cultivate self-knowledge (which again is humility) we will never really be charitable persons. She writes: "I cannot understand how there can be humility without love or love without humility..." (*Way*, 16, 2). Mature prayer and self-knowledge enable us to see that truth in charity and charity in the truth must constitute a life program. Charity of any depth at all requires that we know ourselves.

An important point about Teresian self-knowledge is that it is not introspective or centered in the incomplete self; rather it is God- and Christ-centered. From learning to look at God in truth we discover the truth about the self. "By gazing at [God's] grandeur, we get in touch with our own lowliness; by looking at His purity, we shall see our own filth; by pondering His humility, we shall see how far we are from being humble" (*Castle*, 1, 2, 9). Only in the benevolent presence of the redeeming Lord can we safely descend into the compulsive, wounded, and sinful self. In humility we then find healing, for the Lord is the Master of both the conscious and the unconscious self and can touch the very core of the person, drawing us up into salvation and liberation from all that is contrary to truth and charity. Love of God and love of neighbor both radically depend on authentic self-knowledge. Self-knowledge sees through behavior to its deeper motivation. The genuine desire for such insight leads us to pray to the God of light and to seek out spiritual directors, confessors, and good friends who will tell us the truth about ourselves and keep our prayer life in the light (see *Life*, 13, last part).

Thus self-knowledge is an integral dimension of prayer. We cannot know God without knowing the self and we cannot know the self without knowing God. The fallen self cannot acquire authentic self-knowledge by its own unaided powers. Seeing ourselves in the truth is an aspect of liberation from the fallen self. Again, we need to roam the mansions of self-knowledge all the days of our prayerful lives. Teresian prayer is self-knowing in the light of Christ.

Briefly we should also mention *existential reflection*, i.e., prayerful reflection on life-situations so that we can see and cope with them in the light and love of God. We learn to take our more pronounced states of mind to prayer with us, whether they be due to external or internal causes. It is not that we are encouraging problem-solving at prayer; rather, we learn from Teresa how to draw the presence of Christ into our states of mind and heart. We go to prayer as we are. "If you are experiencing trials or are sad, behold Him on the way to the garden.... He will look at you with those eyes so beautiful and compassionate, filled with tears; He will forget His sorrows so as to console you in yours..." (*Way*, 26, 6).

Affective Prayer and Resolutions. Affective activity is characteristic of Teresian meditation, as we have seen. In the Teresian system, affective prayer is meditation, and all meditation feeds affectivity. Teresa wants the will to desire God, to resolve to serve him, to move toward union with him. Together with "ready-made prayers," she wants us to learn to freely express ourselves with words "that come from...our own heart" (*Way*, 26, 6). Stronger and stronger becomes Teresa's emphasis on affective prayer as she outlines the spiritual journey. For those in the first three dwelling-places she writes: "They would be right if they engaged for a while in making acts of love, praising God, rejoicing in His goodness, that He is who He is, and in desiring His honor and glory. These acts...are great awakeners of the will" and are more important than just following one's "usual meditation" (see *Castle*, 4, 1, 6).

Teresa wants us to move progressively toward affective simplicity because it best prepares for contemplation. (And since in the *Interior Castle* we find no warning about the "passive night of the senses," it may be that Teresian simple affectivity cuts through into initial contemplation without the great adjustment treated by St. John of the Cross.) Teresian affectivity is one of the greatest strengths of her doctrine on meditation.

Let us not neglect *resolutions* as we construct our list of Teresian "methods." Resolutions are very clearly meditative acts that she highly valued. Though Carmelites sometimes spurn this seemingly more "Ignatian" emphasis, Teresa herself is a woman of will. She wants a "very determined determination" to keep on praying all of one's years (see *Way*, 13). And she wants as strong a resolve to grow and pursue virtue as we can manage. We need to cultivate "great desires" for God, and a strong will, a will that will not give up prayer for absolutely anything and that will pursue virtue at all costs. Certainly, Teresian prayer does not require a resolution at each prayer session. But we need to realize that resolutions are a dimension of Teresian affectivity that very concretely relate prayer to real life.

Recollection. Last of all we list the *prayer of recollection.* We refer here to the "active" prayer of recollection, i.e., recollection or rapport with the inner presence of God due to our own meditative efforts.

(Important references include *Life*, 4, 7; 40, 5–6; *Way*, 28–29; *Castle*, 4, 3.) Teresa confesses that until she learned to find the presence of Christ within herself she never knew satisfaction at prayer (see *Way*, 29, 7). "This prayer is called 'recollection' because the soul collects its faculties together and enters within itself to be with its God. And its divine Master comes more quickly to teach it and give it the prayer of quiet than He would through any other method it might use. For centered there within itself it can think about the Passion and represent the Son and offer Him to the Father and not tire the intellect by going to look for Him on Mount Calvary or in the garden or at the pillar" (*Way*, 28, 4). This inward focus is Teresa's favorite orientation for the work of meditation.

So far, then, we have placed Teresian meditation within the larger tradition of monastic prayer, called "lectio divina," and have looked at some basic Teresian notions: mental prayer, vocal prayer, and meditation. We noted that "meditation" in a broad sense is the first category of prayer for Teresa, an active or ascetical stage of prayer just short of contemplation. We have also reviewed the basic characteristics and attitudes underlying Teresian prayer (attentiveness, affectivity, Christ-centeredness, the contemplative orientation of her prayer, the importance of self-knowledge) as well as various Teresian "methods" of praying (e.g., vocal prayer, meditative reading, the use of sacred images for focusing, the employment of interior images, reflection and intuition, affective prayer, resolutions, and active recollection). Now we are ready to apply all these things to the actual practice of prayer, in the context of the rediscovery of Western monastic "lectio divina."

Lectio Divina, Framework of Teresian Prayer

To begin this section on a personal note, until I discovered "lectio divina," my daily practice of prayer took twice as much effort. Now, for many years, I look forward to the time for prayer, and experience not only a greater facility in praying but much greater liberty of spirit. I hope others will experience the same "coming home" in this time-tested prayer of the monastic ages!

We should not be put off by the mention of "monastic" prayer. The monks prayed as simple Christians with the good sense to base their prayer on the sacred Scriptures. What they had that we lack is an ideal environment, the great monastic setting of classical times. But some of us suspect that monastic prayer created the setting before the setting sustained the prayer! You will see how easy the practice is and how the busy meditator of our age can settle down in a short time and enter into the interior castle of deep recollection. We don't always need a quiet place; we need the resolve to be still! It takes a little discipline.

It is not our purpose to discuss the tragic demise of monastic prayer in the West. The fact is that elements of monastic prayer survived, but the basic method was nearly lost even in monastic circles.[6] Teresa was heir to a monastic tradition, but the spirituality of the times was rather thin and a long chain of events over two centuries left the monastic practice of prayer infirm, to say the least. Happily, modern studies in spirituality have revealed again the simplicity and inner unity of monastic prayer. The Teresian spirit feeds and is fed by this rediscovered tradition.

The Elements of "Lectio." "Lectio divina" means literally "the divine reading." It is a monastic designation for the meditative reading of the Scriptures. Its elements are ingredients of a spiritual frame of mind, a holy discipline that intuitively and affectively dwells on a biblical text as a means of seeking communion with Christ. The practice could also be described as dwelling on a scriptural text in the divine presence for the sake of radical change in Christ. Yet again, we could say that "lectio" is making one's own a small selection, phrase, or word of the Bible, in pursuit of greater faith, hope, and charity. In any event, "lectio divina" is prayer over the Scriptures. The monastics of the early and medieval church developed this into a fine art.

The elements are four: 1) *lectio* itself, which means "reading," understood as the careful repetitious recitation of a short text of Scripture; 2) *meditatio* or "meditation," an effort to fathom the meaning of the text and make it personally relevant to oneself in Christ; 3) *oratio*, which means "prayer," taken as a personal response to the text, asking for the grace of the text or moving over it toward union with God; and 4) *contemplatio*, translated "contemplation," gazing at length on something. The idea behind this final element is that sometimes, by the infused grace of God, one is raised above meditation to a state of seeing or experiencing the text as mystery and reality; one comes into experiential contact with the One behind and beyond the text. It is an exposure to the divine presence, to God's truth and benevolence.

A classic exposition of these four elements can be found in *The Ladder of Monks,* a twelfth century monastic letter by Guigo II on the contemplative life, where *lectio, meditatio, oratio,* and *contemplatio* are presented as four rungs leading from earth to heaven.[7] With this work as a general guide, let us consider each element in turn.

Reading. Reading in the monastic tradition involved placing the divine word on the lips. It was a focusing and centering device. One would gently read a selection from the Bible, and when a thought, line, or word stood out and captured the reader's attention, he or she would stop there and dwell on that text, carefully repeating it over and over. At each distraction one would simply return to this repetition. He or she would stay with that same text until it dried up, and would then move on with the reading until finding another engaging text. Classically, the monk would do this repetitious reading out loud, proclaiming the word to his or her own senses, praying with the whole body. This first element is very simple, nothing more than verbal focus on a biblical thought, like placing the word as food in the mouth. In this way monks committed to memory the word of God bit by bit.

Meditation. Once the word of God is on the lips and in the mouth, one begins to bite and chew it; one begins to meditate on it. To meditate means to ruminate, to chew the word, dwelling at leisure on a morsel to extract the meaning of the text. Every word of Scripture was seen as intended for oneself. Every text spoke of Christ and of the pray-er. The monk personalized the text, entering into the meaning and identifying with it. This is the second element of "lectio divina." Meditation employs in an intuitive way all the faculties. One does not work hard at this prayer, but simply keeps listening to the words being repeated, letting them suggest their own images, reflections, intuitive thoughts. The whole process is basically intuitive, a "right-brain" activity (as is said today), like reading a love letter over and over again. Every word is savored and every thought made one's own. (Lovers even memorize their favorite passages!) The meditator ponders and perceives the hidden lessons in the word of God in such a way that wisdom for life is learned. Meditation seeks to acquire the mind of Christ. One slowly begins to see what the scriptures are saying. The meditator begins the lifetime task of hearing the word of God so as to keep it. Meditation is basically *hearing the word* that "lectio" (reading) is repeating.

Prayer. With the help of grace, devout thought engenders *prayer*, the third element of "lectio divina." The word of God moves from the lips to the mind, and now into the heart. "Oratio" or prayer is the response of the heart to the word of God we have heard addressing us through the Scriptures. Basically, prayer in this sense desires the grace of the text so ardently that it demands the needed graces of God. (Guigo II speaks of "imperium," a *command* issued to God from our dire poverty that desperately depends on the salvation only God can give.) Prayer here is the whole affective component of meditation. It is petition, it is affective conversation with sentiments of love, it is resolution to grow in the virtues of Christ, it is compunction of heart for one's sins, it is silent company-keeping, it is the loving gaze. Like the other elements of "lectio," the affective dimension grows and develops. It moves toward simplicity and on into an acquired contemplation. Prayer desires God.

Contemplation. The fourth element is contemplation. Here God slakes the soul's thirst and feeds its hunger, according to Guigo II. God gives the meditator a new wine and lifts him or her above the normal meditative self into the sphere of experienced transcendence. Here at last is an infused element of prayer. Here the Spirit prays in the human spirit. One experiences a state of inner harmony; carnal motions are quieted; the flesh is not at odds with the spirit; the person is in a state of spiritual integration. The light of God's presence shines through the soul experientially. The love of God is no longer abstract, but concretely poured into the receiving self. One can see oneself being loved and loving in return. Clearly, we are speaking of pure gift at this point. These moments can be fleeting or prolonged, subtle or pronounced. They can go and come again. They can mingle with the flow of meditative words repeated, thoughts reflected, intuitions enjoyed, resolutions enacted. But the person is more still and passive; our God is passing by.

We might sum up what Guigo II says of the four elements of "lectio divina" in the following ways: reading seeks; meditation finds (meaning); prayer demands; contemplation tastes (God). Or again: reading provides solid food; meditation masticates; prayer achieves a savor; contemplation is the sweetness that refreshes. Or yet again: reading is on the surface; meditation gets to the inner substance; prayer demands by desire; contemplation experiences by delight.

Injecting the Teresian Spirit into *Lectio Divina*

We began by remarking that there is no distinctively Carmelite or Teresian way to pray. St. Teresa drew from many sources. Nevertheless, Teresa comes out of a tradition deeply influenced by monasticism, and her prayer can be most usefully presented in relation to monastic prayer, now fully rediscovered. What she gives us is a network of notions, attitudes, orientations, and some methods complementary to the basic monastic method of the Western centuries. It is truly easy and delightful to take the Teresian spirit to "lectio divina."

Teresian "Lectio": Reading the Word with Teresa. To practice "lectio" in the Teresian spirit, we begin by extending Teresa's attentiveness to words to our biblical text, reading and repeating what attracts us, with reverence for every word that comes from the mouth of God. Saying the text to ourselves with attention and reverence already makes for mental prayer. Teresa herself found "so much recollection" in the words of the Gospels. Over and over again we center ourself on the word(s), and return to the text at each distraction. We receive each word as it falls from the lips of Christ. He is the one who addresses all of Scripture to the meditator in a most personal way. We ground our prayer in the word of God and feed the presence of God thereby. To remember Scripture is to remember God and Christ. With Carmelites and other Christians the world over, we mutter the "Law of the Lord" [i.e., the Scriptures] to ourselves day and night (see *Rule* of St. Albert, no. 8), and most especially at our more intense sessions of prayer.

Teresian "Meditatio": Meditating with Teresa. While we continue to say the biblical words to ourselves, we listen carefully to their meaning. There is an objective meaning, a literal salvation-oriented meaning intended by the author. And there is an intimate personal meaning, a spiritual sense that applies the text to me. Intuitively I dwell on the words. Either I hear the words coming from Christ to me or I address the words from myself to Christ. I make the biblical words my own, as when I pray a psalm. Meditation makes the words one's own by identification.

Teresa adds a wonderfully helpful ingredient to aid our meditation: the *localization* of God with or within ourselves (or of ourselves within God). She teaches us to think of God as *very near* to us; or as *within* the self, dwelling in the depths; or of the self in God as in one's element (for it is God "in whom we live and move and have our being" [cf. Acts 17:28]). Teresa knows that human beings think spontaneously in terms of time and space. It is extremely helpful to direct our attention to God in some localized place. So we think of God as beside us, in the tabernacle, at the crucifix, or wherever there is a sacred image. With Teresa we go to where God is. She preferred to ponder the divine indwelling, because it is so intimate to think of God within the self. Therefore she recites the words of Scripture to God within, or hears God saying them to her from within the interior castle where he resides in the innermost "dwelling place." But her message is to locate God according to one's own inclination. There is no single way we ought to pray. We pray as we *can*, not as we *ought*. To put words and localized presence together in meditation is typically Teresian.

Teresa gives us another invaluable lesson. Remember how she wants us to pray habitually to Christ, the Way, the Truth and the Life. She would have our prayer be radically Christ-centered. Thus we localize Christ when we pray, addressing our words to him or hearing the divine words of Scripture as *his* words, addressed to us.

We are attentive to both words and presence as Christ's. Christ is the one present and Christ is the one who speaks. Christ the friend keeps us company and Christ the teacher leads us in prayer. This is an important point. In meditation Teresa makes Christ the object of both thought and affection by centering everything about prayer in Christ.

Teresian "Oratio": Prayerful Expression with Teresa. Teresian prayer comes into its own when the heart begins to move. "Oratio" is the response of the heart to the God of the word. The heart can express itself in a million ways, as we have already seen. But here we implement the Teresian principle of making Christ the object of that prayer. And we learn to pray in and through and with him to the Father. With Christ we enter the bosom of the Blessed Trinity and drink in the Spirit from the very source. Teresa expresses the affectionate self to Christ and thereby finds her way to the Father and Spirit. It is a great grace to be fixed on Christ, our companion, our exemplar, our teacher, and our saving mediator. Over the biblical word we relate to Jesus Christ. We find him in every part of Scripture from Genesis to Revelation; in every word we detect his mystery and presence. We relate to God only in Christ. Whether we be at the stage of devout conversation with God, or at the level of simplified company-keeping, we keep our gaze on Christ with Teresa. In his name we make our petitions to himself and to the Father. In him we entertain great desires. In his Spirit we learn to look at him who is looking at us. In him we move toward contemplation.

Teresian "Contemplatio": Contemplating with Teresa. Repetitious reading places the biblical word on the lips. Meditation puts the word in the mind. Prayer takes it to the heart. And then, by the mystical grace of God, contemplation engraves the word in the depths of the spirit. To and fro on the lips, in the mind, in the heart, and in the spirit travels the word of God in personal prayer. With Teresa we have learned to listen both to the words and to the presence. This gentle attentiveness opens us to the subtle influx of contemplative awareness, the gift of God. Slowly an easy facility at prayer becomes ours. We have crossed the obscure borders from meditation to contemplation. At first this contemplation is both subtle and brief. But a new recollection of soul is experienced. We are able to be still at the very core of our being and wait and look and taste and see the presence behind and beyond the words. We encounter the Word himself. We are elevated to know him who knows us through and through. We are elevated to love and be loved in the new energy of the Spirit that prays within us. Here we begin to witness our own transformation as we enter a new illumination. With Teresa we rest in the presence and take a holiday from the work of meditation. We have come to the font of living water and are given to drink freely from the healing source of the Savior.

Conclusion

It is my fervent hope that we will be able to take our experience of prayer and perfect it by employing the Teresian principles of meditation in the context of "lectio divina," the traditional Christian practice of praying over the Scriptures. To be Carmelites, and to be Christians, is to pray out of the past into the ever-evolving present and future. The history of prayer and its development in our own times are essential elements of our prayer methodology. We are traditional souls stretching into the future. We have a long and beautiful heritage that continues to develop and grow. May St. Teresa's breadth of mind and soul become ours and lead us to the renewal of prayer in Carmel and in the Church!

Notes

1. This quotation, with italics added, is taken from *The Collected Works of St. John of the Cross*, trans. Kieran Kavanaugh and Otilio Rodriguez, rev. ed. (Washington, DC: ICS Publications, 1991), p. 97. In earlier editions it appears as *Maxims on Love*, #79.

2. As indicated on p. 6, all quotations from St. Teresa are taken from *The Collected Works of St. Teresa of Avila*, trans. Kieran Kavanaugh and Otilio Rodriguez, 3 vols. (Washington, DC: ICS Publications, 1976–1985).

3. We have looked at St. Teresa's notions of mental prayer, vocal prayer, and meditation. This would also be the logical place to present her notion of contemplation, but we have stopped short of that because our primary interest in this article is meditation.

4. A thorough discussion of Teresian prayer would also need to emphasize its ecclesial, biblical, sacramental, and apostolic dimensions. Here, we simply note that these are all included as aspects of the Christocentric character of Teresian prayer, and in Christ all overlap, to form an existential and incarnational personal stance before God in conjunction with the community of faith.

5. We are more fortunate than Teresa; in Spain during her lifetime vernacular translations of the Bible were forbidden, and only Latin editions were allowed.

6. See the article by Thomas Keating, "Contemplative Prayer in the Christian Tradition: An Historical Perspective," in *Finding Grace at the Center* (Petersham, MA: St. Bede's Publications, 1978), pp. 35–47.

7. Guigo II, *The Ladder of Monks and Twelve Meditations*, trans. with an introduction by Edmund Colledge and James Walsh (Garden City, NY: Doubleday Image, 1978; reprinted Kalamazoo, MI: Cistercian Publications, 1981).

For modern presentations of "lectio divina" see Thelma Hall, *Too Deep for Words: Rediscovering Lectio Divina* (New York, NY: Paulist Press, 1988); Jean Leclercq, "Lectio Divina," *Worship* 58 (May, 1984), pp. 239–248; Jean Leclercq, *The Love of Learning and the Desire for God: A Study of Monastic Culture* (New York, NY: Fordham University Press,

1974), chaps. 1 and 5; Susan Muto, *A Practical Guide to Spiritual Reading* (Denville, NJ: Dimension Books, 1976); and Susan Muto, *The Journey Homeward* (Denville, NJ: Dimension Books, 1977).

One of the best practical guides to "lectio divina" can be found in Chapter X of *Don't You Belong to Me?* by a Monk of New Clairvaux (New York, NY: Paulist Press, 1979).

Questions for Study and Discussion

1. Is there a specific way to practice Teresian or Carmelite prayer?

2. In a few words, describe the spirit of Teresian prayer.

3. What does St. Teresa mean by "vocal prayer"?

4. What does it mean to say that meditation is a category of Teresian prayer?

5. List some of the major characteristics of Teresian prayer.

6. Name some of the methods and acts that qualify as meditative for Teresa.

7. What do we mean when we say that Teresian prayer is self-knowing? Non-introspective?

8. Have you understood what the Western method of "lectio livina" is? Describe its four elements. Do you understand that these elements are not *steps* but rather *ingredients* intermingled to make up the unity of prayer?

9. Take each of the elements of "lectio divina" and inject some Teresian notions into it, to come up with a Teresian "lectio divina."

10. What is meant by the "localization" of God? In what method of prayer proposed by Teresa is the localization of Christ within the self the characteristic note?

11. In what ways has this study enriched your notion of Teresian prayer?

12. Do you perceive the great personal liberty each person has in choosing methods and approaches to prayer?

13. Is it clear that Sacred Scripture, liturgy, and real life should be the tripod upon which one's prayer stands?